Carrying the Cross
with Love 10-31-20

Dear Frankie,
May Jesus continue to bless
you and your family.
Cathy Edwards

Carrying the Cross with Love

Choosing the Grief and Joy of Faith

Cathy Edwards

RESOURCE *Publications* · Eugene, Oregon

CARRYING THE CROSS WITH LOVE
Choosing the Grief and Joy of Faith

Resource Publications
An Imprint of Wipf and Stock Publishers
199 W. 8th Ave., Suite 3
Eugene, OR 97401

www.wipfandstock.com

PAPERBACK ISBN: 978-1-7252-7535-5
HARDCOVER ISBN: 978-1-7252-7536-2
EBOOK ISBN: 978-1-7252-7537-9

Manufactured in the U.S.A.   06/24/20

This book is dedicated to Keith Joseph, who is the light of my life and whose love has brought me closer to the love of my faith in eternal life with Jesus Christ.

Contents

Acknowledgements

First, and foremost, I want to thank Jesus for His unconditional and unfailing love and mercy, which has been a part of me from the time I can remember. Next, my mother, who was the gentlest person I have ever known. Her life was a testimony of her devotion to Mary, and from whom I learned to seek Mary's grace for the intercession of her son, Jesus.

Next, I want to thank the many friends, who are too numerous to mention, in case I omit someone. You know who you are, as we share a love that continues to grow stronger every day. I could not have arrived at the place I am today without your love and support. I especially want to thank my sisters in our bible study group, that have supported my faith, hope and love for almost twenty years. Also, the pastor, music director, and choir members of my church, who have supported me spiritually, musically, and in writing this book.

Last, but certainly not least, I want to thank my family members. My sisters and brother, you have always been there when I needed you and have shared all the sorrows and joys of my life. My aunts, uncles, cousins, nieces and nephews, I have been blessed to know and treasure your presence in my life.

To my husband, Earl, who has been on this journey of love for more than forty years:

You have been, and always will be, my rock. The devotion you show to our family is boundless. You are the only one I would want by my side, for the rest of my life here, and eternally.

Acknowledgements

To my children and grandchildren: Tara, Clayton, Heather, Craig, Holly, Keith, Cameron, Teia, James and Christian: You are the biggest blessings in my life. I am so grateful to know each of your individual personalities, to be included in your lives, to be loved by and love all of you. I pray I have given you the foundation of love for yourselves and your brothers and sisters in Christ, and the knowledge that you are loved by Him now, and forever.

Introduction

I WAS RAISED BY Catholic mother and grandparents in the 1960's, in a much simpler time, and that has been the core of my faith. I have always had a love of Jesus, and as I became a mother, a special place in my heart was opened for Our Lady. When my second son, Clayton, was about five, I had two miscarriages. He had been so excited to think of having a baby sister or brother. I remember him asking me, "Why did the babies die mom?" I answered that maybe something was wrong with their health. He hugged me with tears in his eyes, and replied, "But we would love them no matter what was wrong!" Yes, I thought, we surely would. It filled my heart that he had such tender love and compassion.

We loved being parents so much that we had six children. We concentrated our time, energy, and love on raising them. We had many wonderful adventures of Christmas, summer vacations to the beach, and sharing the daily ups and downs of life. Though at times the days were long, the years sped by. Twenty years passed by in the blink of an eye. Then a major event that changed our lives occurred.

Our youngest child of six, Keith, was born with Down Syndrome, in 2001, and new things began to happen in my life, that caused both great grief and happiness. I knew I wanted to write a book in Keith's honor about the blessings of embracing this special love from this child. The chapters in this book share my story of the gifts given, and the lives enriched, by choosing to love this special child. It is my hope to encourage you, especially if you have a person with a disability in your life, to choose to seek Christ to guide you through the grief you face in your life, by calling out to Him in prayer and obeying His will for you.

More importantly, this book tells the story of God's perfect plan to prepare me to accept His perfect plan with the faith that I can surrender to His will and receive the joy of His perfect love. We all have our crosses to bear in this life, and they are each unique, but God loves us so much that he gives us the choice to carry the cross or put it down. Choosing the cross will not give you a life without suffering, but it will give you and those you love an abundance of blessings. It is written to honor Keith's life, but more importantly, to honor Jesus, in his perfect love for you, who is waiting with open arms, for you to choose Him. It is my story, but it can be your story for eternal joy, in a life with Christ, if you just choose it.

Romans 8:28 (NIH) "And we know that in all things God works for the good of those who love him, who have been called according to his purpose."

A Special Love

2001

KEITH WAS BORN ON April 16, 2001. Since I was almost forty-four, my husband, Earl and I thought our family was complete. However, God had other plans. I had been put on bed rest a week before, which was almost impossible to do, since I had three small children under age six. On April 14, our oldest daughter, Tara, had married her fiancé, Patrick, and I had to listen to the ceremony by phone, as the doctor advised me not to attend. Keith's due date was May 26, and he wanted to prevent going into pre-mature labor.

Earl and Tara had become estranged in their relationship about a year prior to the wedding, when she announced that she and Patrick were going to get married. Earl refused to go to the wedding, since he didn't think Patrick deserved to marry Tara. Of course, what father thinks any man is deserving of his daughter? No matter how much we discussed it, he wouldn't change his mind. Sometimes our biggest assets can be our biggest liabilities as well. He said what he believed, and he believed what he said. If you haven't figured this out yet, Earl is a "cut off your nose to spite your face" type of guy. So, I comforted her and myself with the thought that, well, at least her siblings and I would be there. Now I would not be able to attend either, so only her siblings would be there.

The following day, I noticed that I was not feeling much movement, and just had a strange feeling something wasn't right. After having five children, I knew that even though movement slows down in the third trimester, as the baby gets more crowded, I should still be feeling more movement than I was feeling. I called the doctor and went into his office for a stress test for the baby. He said the baby was under duress, and we needed to go to the hospital to perform a cesarean section right away.

Earl and I drove to Sibley Hospital, in northwest D.C., where we had gone for the five prior births. The doctors prepared for the cesarean, and Earl and I contacted friends and family to ask for prayers. I prayed, *"Lord Jesus, please let this baby be healthy. I know it was your plan to have this child come to* us." In the operating room, the doctors talked to me as they worked, and let me know that the cord had been wrapped around our baby's neck, and it was a good thing I listened to my instinct. They told me it was a boy and whisked him away to clean him up and finish taking care of me. At that moment I was still reeling from how quickly this whole process had taken place and the urgency of safety for my baby and didn't really focus on the news that my baby probably had Down Syndrome. I had previously turned down the amniocentesis test, which is used for screening disabilities in unborn babies, because Earl and I knew we would want to have the baby, even if there was a disability. When the doctor came to do rounds later that evening, he explained to me that they would be sending bloodwork to confirm the diagnosis of Down Syndrome, and it would take about a week for us to obtain results.

When I stayed calm and just said "Okay, thank you", I now realize that he must have thought I was in denial. He asked me to confirm that I understood that my baby probably has Down Syndrome and understood the physical and intellectual disabilities he would have. He also told me the hospital has a support system and someone would be in contact with me soon. I affirmed that I understood. Before he departed, he said to me, "You are very fortunate that this baby has no heart or health issues, and this is a lucky baby boy to have you as his mother." I was not at all concerned about loving this baby boy, but I wasn't sure about my ability to be the best mother he could have.

Earl's strength is being confident in his decisions, which partly comes from needing to be the man of the house, since his dad was not there. My strength is being flexible in the things that life throws at us. I am calm and patient and see the positive in every situation. However, my challenge is to have the confidence in my ability to overcome my fears, especially those dealing with love. I was very blessed to have been able to grow up with my mother and grandparents in their home after my parents' divorce. I was also very blessed to live with my Aunt Theresa, when my grandfather was ill, and the doctors said no children should be living in the house. She was a wonderful second mother to me, and I greatly appreciate her love and care to this day. Still, since my father had not wanted to be a part of my life, and I lived apart from my mother for a time when I was a young child, combined with being an overly introverted and sensitive child, I had never fully resolved these issues. As issues do, these kept bubbling to the surface in moments of crisis.

I was also concerned about Earl having the same immediate feelings of love that I had, since I had carried Keith inside for nine months and already loved him. These worries I had would prove to be valid, but little did I know how God had already planned the path we would take, in order to arrive at the answers only He could provide. My faith kept bringing me back to God for help and comfort.

When Earl came to visit that evening, and I gave him the news from the doctor, he was devastated. He broke down with shock and grief that the life he imagined with this baby boy was not to become a reality. He could not imagine that there could be anything wonderful about this unexpected change in our lives. We sobbed together that night, consoling one another as best we could. Although we clung to the hope that the test results may come back negative, in our hearts we knew the truth.

The next morning, I had already begun to move on, in the daily care for our new family member. Earl seemed unable to lift himself out of his depression, barely able to complete the daily rituals of working, eating and sleeping. After several weeks, I was worried about him, and exhausted from lack of sleep and caring for 4 young children. I approached him about going to talk to someone, but he refused. Privacy had always been important to him, and he was not ready to share this event with the world.

We had always been able to communicate well with each other and had made it a point to have a date night every week, to make sure we stayed connected in our marriage. Both of our sets of parents had divorced, and we knew from our own experience how difficult it was on the children. Still, I felt like I was carrying this burden alone and worried about our marriage as well. The impact this had on our marriage was harder for me than caring for Keith. I was worried about not being the best mom for Keith. How could God think I was the one for this job?! I was even more angry at Earl for not staying connected to me during this huge change in our lives. How did he think I could do this alone?!

One night, when I was in bed trying to sleep, I thought, *I am so alone, and I cry out to God to help me. I feel a warmth flow from the top of my head to my toes and know God is telling me not to be afraid because he is with me. I only need and take one day at a time with Keith, and love him, the same as I do with my other five children.* It was an experience I had never had and was so comforting.

Of course, as I was going through my own emotions, Earl had emotions of his own. After beginning to lift out of his depression, he began praying to God more. He realized how he couldn't assume that we would all continue our lives as we had planned each day and decided to reach out to Tara to reconcile their relationship. I was filled with joy at this news and had the first inkling that Keith was going to be a part of making some wonderful things happen in our lives and lives of others.

We both began to realize that Keith was put here exactly as God intended for him to be and had plans for him as well, though it would still be awhile until Earl fully realized the special love Keith was given by God and would give to others. We would not understand until later that this meant that only by letting go of our control, accepting our grief and the many challenges that lay ahead, could we claim the joy and love it brought.

On September 11th, the tragedy of this nation brought us to our knees, as we realized again the fragility of life, and the loss of our control over the conditions in life. It was another time of appreciating each moment that allows us to be with our loved ones. In addition to this event, Earl lost a fellow police officer in the line of duty. Our Thanksgiving and Christmas this year was filled with thankfulness and love, with a special appreciation for living life fully each moment of every day.

What it boiled down to for both of us was that our strengths and weaknesses required both of us to let go of the control we clung to so desperately. We needed to realize that God is the one who has control. We never have and we never will, and the sooner we accept this and release our control, the sooner we can truly live our lives in the way God intended us to do.

One of the biggest gifts God has given to each of us is freedom of choice. Earl and I have made many choices that were mistakes and sins, just like every person does. We will all continue to make mistakes and sin, because we are all human beings. We have also been given many blessings, just as all people have been blessed. Sometimes when we are in pain or grieving, it is hard to appreciate those blessings in those moments, but they are still there. We have a choice to embrace the blessings or focus on the pain, and a choice whether to do it alone, or with God's support. He has already forgiven us for our sins by dying on the cross, and we can receive his grace simply by accepting Him as our Redeemer and loving Him.

As I reflect upon the biggest blessing of my life here on earth, it is being blessed with my six children and my grandchildren. Since they are my biggest blessing, they are the part of my life that it has been most difficult to turn over to God. There have been so many times in my life when I have worried about them, that I have had to remind myself that they really are God's children. Earl and I have been blessed to borrow them by the grace of God.

When I think of how much I love my children, I think of how much God loves us, who are his children. I think of how much he loves his son, Jesus. He has shown how much he loves us, by having him come to earth to die on a cross for our sins. The bible verse that tells us so beautifully the extent of God's love, is as stated in John 3:16 "For God so loved the world, that he gave his only begotten son, that whosoever believeth in him should not perish, but have everlasting life."

Though you have already met Keith, I'd like to share some things about each of our children with you before we go any further in this book, so that you can get to know them a little bit and understand how God worked through each of them. I also hope that you can share in my joy, as you also share in my grief. Perhaps you can reflect on the blessings and joys of your life and share them with someone else.

We chose to name our children with a first name that has to do with nature, one of God's most beautiful and most encompassing creations. It is incredible to realize the power and tenderness of the rain, snow and sun. The power of a tsunami, yet tenderness of a drop of dew on a blade of grass; the power of an avalanche cascading down a mountain, yet tenderness of each unique snowflake as it falls on a tree branch and glistens with prisms from the rainbow; the power of a volcanic eruption, yet tenderness of the suns' rays caressing a flower as it stretches to greet it.

We also chose to name our children with a middle name from a saints' name, that reflected our admiration of that saint and honored the name of a family member who had passed. Heather's name was very special to me, because I prayed to Mary after my second miscarriage, if she blessed me with the gift of another child, if it was a girl, I would make Mary her middle name.

Our oldest child, Tara Michelle, is the most loyal child, sibling, friend, wife or mother anyone could have. She has the most positive attitude of appreciation of whatever the moment brings. She is a musician, a teacher, an athlete, patient, and kind. Her husband, Patrick is adventurous, intelligent, courageous and steady. He is patient, and musical. He is a trusted friend, husband, son, and father. We are so blessed to have him as a son. They are both great parents to Cameron and James.

Our oldest son, Clayton Matthew is a wonderful combination of tenderness and spitfire. He loves a good debate. I remember one day we were discussing some topic we had different opinions about, and I finally threw my hands up and said, "You just like to argue!" He immediately yelled back "I do not!" We both had a good laugh with that one. He is an athlete, a musician, a police officer, has a great sense of humor, hates for the part of life that he is loving to have to end. He loves his siblings so much that he once told me he couldn't imagine loving anyone more, until he met his wife Ann, and had his own children, Teia and Christian. Ann has become another daughter to us, and is a wonderful wife, mother and friend. Shortly after we met, she said to me, "Thank you for loving Clayton so much." He loves Jesus.

Heather Marie is the beautiful combination of being fragile and determined. She is courageous and hardworking to go after her dreams, and she attains them. When she tells you her opinion, it is always honest. She watches after her three younger siblings so well that she has earned the nickname "Minnie Mommy". She adores Keith and is his guardian, along with Earl and I. When she met her fiancé, Clay, it was a package deal that if he was marrying her, he needed to want to have Keith be with them when the time comes that Earl and I can no longer care for him. He passed the test with flying colors when he took the ten—hour ride to the beach with us, sitting in the back seat of the car between Heather and Keith, and Keith loved him. We are thrilled they are marrying in a few months, and that he will officially be part of our family. She loves Jesus.

Craig Anthony is the son who fully lives in the present moment, without regretting the past or worrying about the future. He is an athlete, Keith's hero, working towards becoming a police officer. He is calm, kind, and patient. He is willing to work hard to achieve his goals. He loves Jesus.

Holly Catherine has such a tender heart for people and for animals. She is introverted. She is one of the most talented people I know. She is musical, intelligent, athletic, artistic, and creative. She loves Jesus.

You will hear a lot about our youngest son, Keith Joseph, in the following chapters. He loves people, animals, swimming, cheeseburgers, cupcakes and music, and is great at technology. He is loved and loves with innocence and trust. He loves Jesus.

I have left off the individual names of people (other than family) and places I mention in the book, in order to respect their privacy. I think the people who have been such an important part of my life will know I am speaking of them as I describe certain events, and know that is my way of acknowledging thanks for the support and love they have given to me and to my family. It is important that we all have loved ones to share the good and bad in our lives, and to feel supported and loved. As you give the gift of support to others, also allow yourself to receive the gift of support from others.

I learned many prayers and hymns from the time I was a small child until the present, between attending services and singing in choirs. When I decided this was the time I should be writing this book, I also thought it would be appropriate for me to include some quotations from the bible, some prayers and some hymns that have been especially meaningful and helpful to me over the years of challenges. They have helped me to appreciate that Jesus is with me and to draw strength from his Divine mercy and grace. I am going to add these throughout the book, at the end of each chapter, so that it is easier for you to return to later. I pray that they will be helpful to you as well. All the prayers are either my own prayer, or I have listed the title of tradition Christian prayers in quotation marks.

Prayer: Lord Jesus, Help Me.

Song: "Prayer of the Norwegian Child" by Richard Kountz

Bible quote: 2 Corinthians 12:9 "My grace is sufficient for you, for my power is perfected in weakness" It is through our weakness (darkness) that the power (light) of Christ shines most brightly.

2

Back to School

2002

As our new routine settled in, the days seemed to be extremely long, with additional doctor visits, physical therapy and speech therapy visits, but the weeks and months flew by. Keith reached all the milestones of a typical baby, but they were delayed, and somehow that made it even sweeter, as he was cheered by his siblings. I had not returned to teaching, and was working part-time as a cantor, soloist, and section leader at our neighborhood Catholic Church and teaching private piano lessons in the community. One of the mothers of my students decided to take lessons as well, and we often chatted before or after their lessons about how the lessons were progressing and how things were going in the family.

One day, the mother turned to me and asked, "Would you be interested in joining in our bible study group?" Even though I had been Catholic all my life and had been surrounded by Gospel readings and sermons containing bible scripture, I had never studied the bible before. I have always loved learning new things and knew what a loving person she was, so I eagerly accepted the invitation.

We rotated houses and met bi-weekly, with guided studies on books of the bible, or through bible study sessions written by Christian leaders. There were five of us, and it was a comfortable fit for me. This motivated me to begin praying every morning, and this routine became my favorite part of the day, where I could peacefully rest in the love of Jesus. Somehow knowing the rest of the day would bring total chaos felt just a little bit easier, knowing I could return to my peacefulness the next morning.

I have continued with this prayer routine and this bible study group for almost nineteen years now, and it has been the most important stepping-stone for me to develop a personal relationship with Christ. Every person can have this blessing, if they choose to make the time and effort to incorporate this into the day. For me, the first thing in the morning worked best, but for others in our group, they chose other times of the day, such as when kids were at school, or lunchtime at work or before bed. Some of us preferred structured prayer, others benefited from personal dialogue, and some of us used both methods. It is like anything else you do, in that, the more you practice, the better you become.

Since we all stayed praying together for so long, we also developed a strong support system. Over the many years together, we have shared the joys and sorrows of our lives with prayer, conversation, hugs, food and whatever else a bible study sister and their family needed. One of our sisters had breast cancer as a young mother, and it returned after she joined our group, and she was taken to heaven, so there is one empty spot that we won't be able to fill until we are reunited in heaven. Still, we have had other sisters come and go over the years, and we now have nine sisters in our group.

Working with Keith on his special challenges motivated me to return to school to get my master's in special education. I applied and was accepted to George Mason University, where I began taking Intro to Special Education. I felt like I would only be able to take one class at a time, for time, energy and financial reasons, but was looking forward to the journey.

The professor of this class informed us that there was a new program beginning at Mason called the LIFE Program. The acronym stood for Looking into Future Environments. The program offered free tuition but required fifteen hours of teaching classes to young adults with special needs, who were attending Mason to get life and career experience and would receive a certificate of completion when they graduated. I was excited to begin this program, and though it took me five years to complete, it was a wonderful experience, where I taught reading and music appreciation classes and students performed an end of year program.

I had always loved young children, but it gave me a better understanding and passion for working with young adults with disabilities. I especially enjoyed seeing the confidence these young men and women achieved, as they reached the dreams that they had been unsure they could achieve. I also enjoyed collaborating with staff and families. Just as I had discovered with Keith, that I thought I would be the one teaching him so much, when he taught me so much more, these students re-affirmed the same thing. *Through prayer and reflection, I realize Keith is a special child, sent from God to do His mighty works.* I was amazed that because God had allowed me to glimpse how special Keith was, I was able to use this realization to improve my ability to help him, myself, and now even outside of my small world, into an area to benefit others. I truly sensed that the Holy Spirit was actively guiding us and began seeking for signs of what I was called to do, in order to obey God's will for me.

You, too, can watch for signs that God sends you. Through pray and reflection, God will send you his messages, but oftentimes it is sent in his timing, and not always the answer we want to hear. Sometimes we may pray and feel our prayers are not answered, but he always hears us. He makes the choice that is best for us, not that is quickest or easiest for us. With practice, we can improve our ability to recognize his answers and trust ourselves to make the choice to obey his will. When we do, we are blessed by his grace and mercy.

Prayer: Lord, send the Holy Spirit to guide me, so that I may know and obey your will.

Song: "The Prayer" by David Foster, Carole Bayer Sager, Tony Renis, Corey Hart and Alberta Testa

Bible quote: Philippians 4:13 "I can do all things through Christ who gives me strength."

3

Life Goes On

2003–2007

MEANWHILE, I AM COMPLETING schoolwork, teaching private lessons, and working at church as cantor, section leader and soloist. Keith is a happy baby, growing to a toddler and then a little boy. His innocence makes him endeared to everyone he knows. However, I need to have eyes in the back of my head to keep him and everyone around him safe. He begins grabbing/hitting children, more to get a reaction from them than to hurt them, but sometimes they are hurt. It is so embarrassing when your child reaches over and hits another child who is a stranger, and the mom glares at you like you have three heads. I begin saying a prayer every time we go outside in the community *"God, please let Keith stop hitting other children so he can have friends, and I can enjoy letting him and others be safe and happy."* This prayer is repeated over and over but is not to be answered for years.

I join a weekly parent support group that is led by a social worker through the Infant Toddler group in Fairfax County. It is very helpful in realizing I am not in this alone. Sometimes the questions are answered and there is a solution to a problem. Mostly it is a relief to know that though most people I know aren't going through this, at least there are some people in the world that "get it" when I talk to them. Though I have always been respectful to people, and had friends, it is a time that I looked at who I chose to spend my time and energy to sustain a relationship. If I met someone who was in a totally different place with their outlook on life, I was polite, but didn't attend to cultivate a true friendship.

The challenges continue, but so do the rewards. In 2005, my daughter, Heather who is eleven, writes a story called "A Special Kind of Hero", for the Reflections Contest at school. She wins the contest and we are all so proud of her. Earl and I are also able to realize the positive effect of compassion that Keith is spreading to his siblings. Heather will end up deciding to go into the Special Education field.

Keith loves to play in the water but keeps getting ear infections. He is also having difficulty hearing the high-pitched tones. The doctors and therapists recommend he has tubes placed in his ears, which we do. This does reduce the amount of ear infections and he seems to hear better too. Speech therapists and physical therapists come to visit the house weekly for two years, and some progress is made. They also recommend getting a dog for improving socialization and speaking skills. We get a chocolate lab puppy, and name him Major. He quickly becomes a part of our family.

At age three, Keith is eligible to attend pre-school through the county program at our community school. Keith thrives in this environment, where he loves his teacher and the socialization with other students. However, he still hits other children impulsively, for no apparent reason. I work with the entire team, developing and implementing strategies to help with this, and some days it works and some days it doesn't work.

He does things like pull the fire alarm at school and run up to the front of the church to start playing on the piano in the middle of the service. We nickname him "Houdini", because he is physically flexible and visually smart. He figures out how to get out of any safety device we put him in, including a crib, a car-seat, a highchair, and more. He is also acutely aware of people around him. He watches what they are doing, listens to what they say, and watches body language, especially looking people in the eyes, to see if they mean what they say and if they truly care about him. He almost has a sixth sense about people's character.

In 2006, when Keith is five, it is time for him to leave this pre-school program and begin kindergarten. There is not a special education class at his school, so the team decides to try the general education classroom, making modifications to accommodate his disabilities. It is a disaster. The noise and lack of strict routine and consistency brings more and more hitting episodes. This is a sign Keith requires more support. At his Individualized Education Plan (IEP) meeting, the team decides it would be the best placement for him to attend another elementary school that has a special education classroom, with the additional support necessary to help him be successful.

Keith starts saying the name of his pre-school teacher to me many times a day. I respond, "I know you miss your teacher. It's OK. You have a new teacher and new friends now." However, Keith has different ideas about the transition! One morning, when I am working in the kitchen, in the room next to the living room where he is playing, it suddenly is very quiet. We recently have been playing games of hide and seek at home, so I think at first maybe he has hidden somewhere. I walk around the house, looking for him and calling his name.

After a few minutes, I begin to get annoyed and call his name "Keith! Time to come out now!" When there is no response, I call again "Keith! You win! I can't find you. Come out NOW!" Dead silence. I look outside. We live in a cul-de-sac with a pipe-stem. I go outside and start running toward the street.

I am frantic now, and just about to turn home and make some calls for help, when a man driving by in a car sees the look on my face. He yells out, "Are you looking for a little boy with blond hair?" I reply "Yes!" He points around the corner and says, "He was rushing up the street there!" I whisper to myself, *"Lord Jesus, please help me find my little boy. Let Keith be safe!"* While frantically searching for Keith, who was only five years old, with Down Syndrome, who was outside somewhere by himself, my heart was in my throat.

I jump into my car and take off in the direction of the school, which is only three blocks away. I see him right as he is about to turn into the entrance to the school. I scoop him up and hug him like there's no tomorrow. I sob with tears of relief that he is safe and yell, *"Praise God! Thank you, Jesus!"* This is one time my prayers were answered immediately, and I couldn't have been more grateful.

When he ran away at age five because he missed his preschool teacher, I should have known to listen when he kept calling her name to me. That if I wasn't going to take him to see her, he'd just get there himself. This would happen again many times when he was growing up. He knew what he wanted and while he couldn't always verbalize it, or if he verbalized it and didn't get it, he would act on it by himself. I learned to really listen when he was telling me something. While frantically searching for Keith, who was only five years old, with Down Syndrome, who was outside somewhere by himself, my heart cried out *"Lord Jesus, help me!"* The Lord Jesus did help me, yet again, as I cried tears of relief.

Keith's teacher at his new school, is a wonderful teacher and person. It takes some time, but Keith settles in the following school year and has a great time learning and following safety rules most of the time through his elementary school years. She tutors him when he moves on to middle school and we develop a family friendship, where she joins us for his birthday celebrations.

Though it is hard work, I enjoy teaching at Mason and completing my classes. I learn so much that will be helpful in working with students and with Keith. What I learn with Keith helps me with my students, and what I learn working with my students is sometimes helpful with Keith as well. It is a win-win for me.

I complete my classes in May of 2007 and graduate. I apply to Fairfax County School system and get an interview for a special education teacher position at a high school in Fairfax County. I am hired!

Prayer: "Glory Be"

Song: "Abide with Me" by William Henry Monk and Henry Francis Lyte

Bible quote: Isaiah 41:10 "Do not fear, for I am with you; do not be dismayed, for I am your God. I will strengthen and help you; I will uphold you with my righteous hand."

4

School Stories for All

2007

I COMPLETE MY DEGREE and I begin teaching at Fairfax High School. Keith begins first grade. His shenanigans continue, but everyone is patient, as he is so young and has a disability. At the same time, anxiety for my daughter, Holly, gives her panic attacks that are debilitating to the point that she stops playing sports and refuses to go to school. We look at bible quotes together, to see if there is a short quote she can memorize and say to herself to help ease her anxiety. Holly selects Philippians 4:13.

Holly and I pray together "I can do all things through Christ, who gives me strength." She will pray this prayer hundreds of times, both alone and with me, as she works through the panic attacks. I remember one time, where, I realized how overwhelming this had become for her. She was playing in a soccer game, and started having a panic attack, and just whispered to the coach as she ran off the field, "I don't feel well!" But she kept running and stayed away long enough that I had no idea where she had gone. My friend noticed and stepped aside with me and took my hand. She said "It's OK, Cathy, that you aren't with her. She has Jesus with her. Let's say a prayer!" We did pray, and it calmed me down. Holly returned shortly, and I remember thinking, I need to remember this next time she has a panic attack.

Since I am working at our neighborhood school, where Holly attends school, I am able to get her back into the building by telling her she just needs to attend school every day, and if she needs to take breaks or come to my classroom during lunch, we can work that out. We talk with her teachers and her counselor and have a support system in place for her. I realize it is no accident that I am working at the same school she attends , especially since this puts me in a place where I am emotionally and physically able to be there to help Holly.

It was especially surprising that of all my children, she had the panic attacks. She was the child who, on her first day of kindergarten, smiled, said goodbye and turned her back to run into class. She was the child who was so confident, she would ask her older brother, "How come I can do this, and you can't?" She was a child who was so gifted in so many areas: sports, music, art and writing. Her confidence was unlimited—until her first panic attack happened. It literally took her breath away and shook her world. It shook my world, too, and broke my heart to see her just shut down to a shell of herself.

I make an appointment with a family counselor at a Wellness Center, so Earl, Holly and I can begin a support system at home. We leave for the first appointment, and Holly refuses to go in when we get to the office. She tells me that talking about it makes it feel more "real" and "true" and sets off more panic attacks. I remind her that she felt that way at school, too, but it got better. I tell her that sometimes things get worse before they get better, and this happens to everyone in their life. She finally agrees to go in, but says "I'll go in, but I'm not going to say anything. It will make me have a panic attack if I start thinking about it and talking about it."

We go in, and she mostly listens at the first session. As sessions continue, she begins to build a rapport with the counselor, and starts talking more. She is diagnosed with Attention Deficit Disability (ADD), which we learn, is more common in children with a lot of creativity. We also learn that they also have anxiety more often than typical children. We begin using strategies and it does improve enough to take the edge off, but not enough to live a typical life, so we decide to add medication to see if that helps bring her back to the real Holly. This does seem to be the best solution for her right now. She will battle these panic attacks for many years.

School seems to settle in for Holly the following year, and she realizes she misses sports, but doesn't want the pressure of playing on the basketball team at school. We begin looking into other sports teams on which she can play. One day we are in our grocery store, and we run into the basketball coach she had in elementary and middle school. She asked Holly what she was doing at school and in sports, and though Holly was glad to see her, she didn't have much to reply.

As Holly continued shopping around the store, I quickly updated her coach on what was going on. She mentioned to me that Holly should come to watch a practice at Slam City, where she works with someone who is a great coach and great person. Holly went and decided to start training and playing again. I was so impressed as I watched the practices, where they began with a prayer, and where the players supported one another.

This was another moment I realized that seeing our friend at Giant was not just a coincidence. This was awesome, because he is a Christian, and started every practice with a prayer. Yet, he was a tough trainer and intended for the kids to win their games. It was exactly the balance she needed to move forward. It would help Holly get back her physical strength and confidence to play again. She would work for Coach, coaching basketball to young children. She would also try out and make the varsity basketball team at Westfield. But this is way down the road.

Prayer: "Our Father" (The perfect prayer given by Jesus)

Song: "You Are Mine"—David Haas

Bible quote: 1 Peter 5:7 "Cast all your anxiety on him because He cares for you."

5

The Runner

2008–2009

MY SON CRAIG IS finally diagnosed as a student with learning disability (LD). Though we have known it for years, his sixth-grade teacher realized Craig would be more successful as he entered middle school, if he received some academic support. She set up a team meeting, where we put a 504 plan in place, that would provide extra time to complete work or reduced length of assignments. He can finally get the extra time to complete work at grade level and be successful in his academics. He is the type of student who often gets overlooked, because he has good behavior and he is a hard worker. He can complete the schoolwork he is given, but it takes him twice as long, due to a processing disability.

Keith runs away from home for the second time, simply because he thinks about how fun it would be to take our dog, Major, outside with him, one summer morning at about 5 a.m. His siblings all hop on bikes looking for him, while I drive in the car. *On the way, I am praying over and over. My chant is "Lord Jesus, protect Keith."* After about ten minutes of not finding him, I called the police to help. The officer says, "Yes, we have a little boy and a dog here we just picked up and brought to the station. Come over and get them." When we get to the station, the policeman tells us

0

our dog, Major, was not going to let Keith into his car, unless he was able to sit right next to him. In this prayer of praise, I loudly proclaim *"Praise Jesus! God is good!"*

After this second incident of Keith leaving the house unattended, we decide we need to put locks on the doors. We purchase some chains to put across the tops of the doors, from the inside, so Keith can't reach them and walk outside alone. This running away is typical in children with autism, and we will see it happen several more times as Keith is growing up. It seems to stem from his impulsivity after having a thought, and acting on it, without being able to consider safety or appropriateness first.

We consider talking to his IEP team about adding autism to his diagnosis, but we realize that his primary diagnosis is Intellectual Disability (ID) and adding another label won't change anything. We just needed to be sure to indicate Keith's impulsivity and history of running away when others were working with him.

Keith is a visual learner. He learns best academically by pictures and symbols, especially if they contain the added element of music. He learned to read by having a picture symbol with the main words, and then gradually withdrawing the symbol until he recognized the word alone. He remembers which direction we drive when going to his favorite places and calls out when he wants us to change our direction. When we purchase a car DVD player, he is looking over dad's and big brother Craig's shoulder to correct them in the installation process. He is giving directions "No, push this button." Darned if he isn't correct!

He is also very good at recognizing when a person care about him and when they don't. He will do a much better job listening to a person who he knows is telling him something because they care. He will sometimes antagonize someone just to get a reaction and see if they stay calm. It is almost as if he has the capability to see inside a person's heart and soul. It is a gift not many people have.

Prayer: Lord Jesus, be with me

Song: "Be Not Afraid" John Michael Talbot

Bible quote: Proverbs 3:5 "Trust in the Lord with all your heart, and lean not on your own understanding"

6

Heaven on Earth: Jill's House

2010

WHEN KEITH WAS NINE, and in fourth grade, I heard about the wonderful respite center in McLean. Of course, even at his tender age, he has gotten thrown out of every group he has participated: School, summer-school, therapeutic recreation, and on and on. Of course, when he can't keep himself and everyone else safe, it is understandable. Since this new place is a place specifically for children with special needs, and it is based from McLean Bible Church, a Christian place (though I will later learn it does not require families to be Christian, nor does it attempt to recruit families to Christianity, it simply and beautifully lives the love of Christ through care of these children), just maybe he can be successful there?

Fortunately for us, this is a well-kept secret right now. We complete the application process, and he begins attending Jill's house. He will stay a weekend every month. The first weekend, I don't think I slept a wink, worrying about how he was doing and wondering if I was going to get a call. It didn't take us long to realize we had found the little heaven on earth for Keith and for us. The only place he can go outside of the home, where he is loved and safe, and we are allowed rest. We can do things alone or with another family member, fully enjoy each moment and anticipate the return to the demands in our world.

The first weekend drive home, Keith just gazed out the window, turning to look back at Jill's House, as if he couldn't believe what a fun time he had just had and what a neat place it was. Later, at home, he offered some details about what he did. He loved swimming in the pool, the computer station, the music room and playground. As time progressed, he offered more and more details, such as particular staff he enjoyed and friends he played with. A detailed page of food and drink consumed, activities enjoyed, staff who cared for Keith and any observations was sent home.

One of the things that children with special needs miss out on is playing with friends. Though kids in school are becoming more aware about including them in activities at school, they are rarely invited to homes or outings in the community. This respite provided this additional opportunity, in addition to keeping our children safe and giving us a respite.

It opened many doors for the entire family, including having our daughter Heather take a position on the staff, where she proclaimed when she came home "Mom, I've never been in a place where you can work and feel so much love at the same time. You can just feel the energy of love when you walk in!" Though the staff never taught lessons about Jesus, they didn't need to, because they taught it through their actions. It motivated her to get her degree as a special education teacher and she has been teaching in Fairfax County for the past several years. Earl, Heather and I have guardianship for Keith, and it is so comforting to know that some day when Earl and I can no longer care for him, Heather, and her fiancé, Clay, will be the ones who care for him.

The two staff members who run the family support program there are two of the most amazing people. They both are so professional, but always go the extra mile in providing support for the entire family with retreats, support group meetings and respite. We come to know two staff members who worked at Jill's House and have become both caregivers for Keith at home and personal family friends, because they actually look forward to being with Keith and enjoy all his challenges as well as all of his innocence.

As Keith became more and more comfortable coming to Jill's House, he began to count down the days until he was going. Once we got to ten days until he could go, he would wake up every morning and say, "Nine days mom." and his face would light up with a big smile, until we got to the day he was going. He would do impulsive things there, such as flush a sock down the toilet, throw his toothbrush up exactly in the crack of the ceiling where it would be stuck, hide in the utility closet, sneak DVD's he liked into his bag to bring home, and change the settings on all the computers to a different color or different language. One time, Heather recalled the staff calling on the walkie-talkie "Can someone please change the monitors on all the computers back to normal settings?!" and she knew it must have been Keith. Still, he knew he was loved no matter what he did or didn't do. Isn't this unconditional love what every person wants and deserves in their life?

Most importantly, it inspired Earl to accept Christ as his Savior, which I had been praying for thirty years. There is a program called Access Ministry at McLean Bible Church, next door to Jill's House. The staff cares for children with disabilities so the family can attend a peaceful service. They also teach the children about the love of Jesus and do activities with them. Earl, our children and I decided to try this one Sunday. Earl loved the history and geography that was discussed and personality of the pastor, Lon Solomon. After attending for a while, he accepted Christ as his Savior. He had believed in God but was not sure about Christ. This was a huge event for our family that we celebrated. Our innocent little boy, Keith and God's timing were an answer to persistence in prayer and faith in God's perfect timing.

When I was asked at one event to speak about how Jill's House has impacted our family, my first thought was "Jills House is heaven on earth." It is the closest to perfect that any place could be on earth, because it is filled with the love of Jesus. The works of the Holy Spirit are so evident. When I thought of retiring from teaching students with special needs, and obtaining a job at Jill's

House, I knew I had to wait to work there until Keith aged out and couldn't attend any more. There was no way I could take this gift away from him. We all hate to think about him losing this opportunity when he turns twenty-two in a few years.

Prayer: Let every thought, word, and deed be done in your honor and glory, Lord.

Song: "Amazing Grace"—John Newton

Bible quote: Genesis 1:21 "God created every living thing, and God saw that it was good."

7

Overwhelmed

2011–2012

I AM GETTING CALLS from Keith's school almost every day, saying that I need to leave work and pick up Keith. He is hitting other students and adults, going to the bathroom on the floor, pulling down his pants, and knocking furniture all over the classroom. I am exhausted, but I still realize how fortunate I am for all the support in my life. I realize that the hormone surge is causing an increase in the impulsivity, and Keith doesn't know how to handle it, so it is manifesting in his behaviors.

The school team and I have many conferences, meetings, and try many strategies, but nothing seems to make much change in his behavior. Middle school is difficult for all children, with raging hormones, and only two years to adjust to the transition of a new school, teachers and friends. By the time they adjust the second year, it's time to prepare to move on to high school. It is especially difficult for a student with a disability, who needs consistency and emotional stability.

I transfer to teach at our neighborhood school. I am so happy that I will be working where my children attend high-school, and that my commute is short. My first year there, I meet a co-worker who is filled with the love of Jesus. We begin a friendship that continues to this day to be mutually supportive personally and spiritually. We begin to pray every morning together before school begins, and gradually, several other staff members request to come pray. We pray for the guidance in teaching and supporting our students and their families. We pray for wisdom in collaborating with staff. We pray for the health and happiness of everyone.

My second year, I am asked to be the team leader for our department, and even though this is an additional responsibility I do not need during this already challenging time with Keith, I feel like it would be disrespectful to our department chair to say no, so I agree. Though most of the team are kind and professional, I begin to feel a growing evil presence in a few of the staff members, who resist any assistance and direction I attempt to give to the team, both vocally and by email. I hear that two of the staff are unhappy that we pray together, and resentful that the position was requested of me rather than for one of them.

I know I need to address it with one staff member, but I must do so from both love and strength of Jesus. I pray *"Jesus, please send the Holy Spirit to give me guidance and courage to say the right words to send away this evil presence."* I go and speak with this staff member in person. She, who has acted with such aggression toward me by arguing vocally and by email with every action I take to support the team, breaks down sobbing when I address my concerns with her.

With the grace of the Holy Spirit, this evil spirit is sent away, and there is a positive change in the department. It gets back to me that the comment was made. "I didn't think she had it in her." The other staff member had commented that she didn't think I had the nerve to address the situation directly. What she didn't realize is that, it wasn't my own strength. I was able to draw strength from Jesus. Jesus had given me the strength to address it, in order to get rid of the negative energy that was among the whole staff and affecting care of our students. The important thing was to replace it with positive love from Jesus.

In Keith's second year of middle school, I take him to a psychiatrist, and we begin some new strategies and medication to see if this helps reduce the impulsivity. What made me decide to try the medication was because I could see how overwhelmed Keith was by feeling so out of control. I sensed this was going to be a long ride, that would take a combination of time of hormones settling down and strategies beginning to help. We were in a survival mode for this school year, but I prayed that next year when he began high school, things would improve.

Caregivers' Prayer: (author unknown) Lord of all, help me to be flexible and have the ability as I care for my child with disabilities. I pray I would not get angry when things don't go as planned. Fill me with your peace. Help me to discover the humor in situations. May I be overflowing with your joy. Give me strength, this day. But most of all, heavenly father, I want my child to know he/she is loved. Thank you for your amazing unconditional love. May I love like you love. In Jesus's name. Amen.

Song: "Turn Your Eyes Upon Jesus" by Helen Howarth Lemmel

Bible quote: Isaiah 30:21 "Your ears will hear a voice behind you saying, "This is the way. Walk in it.""

8

My Earthly Mother
and Heavenly Mother

2013–2014

My mother, who was born in 1924, was the gentlest person I have ever known. As she aged, and I began to realize some day she would die, I knew I would miss having her as my mother and the most beautiful friend anyone could have. She began smoking in her twenties, when the harmful effects of nicotine where unknown by the general population. She divorced my father after many years of enduring his alcoholism, womanizing, gambling and abandonment. She had 4 children to care for, and even working full-time, she could not make enough to keep us surviving. Fortunately, her parents welcomed her to their home, and we grew up in that loving and stable home.

My grandparents, Grampa and Danna were Catholics, and we all attended Catholic school and mass from the time we moved in with them, when I was a toddler. Grampa and my Uncle Bill were my father figures and provided both love and guidance. My Uncle Bill is still alive, and still is an important part of the whole family, as patriarch. When my Grampa began having a series of heart attacks, I went to live with my mom's sister, Aunt Theresa, who was also caring and gentle. She is still alive, is the matriarch and continues to be like a second mother to me.

In our home, God, family and country were important. Academics and music were stressed. My grandfather was a pharmacist and played cello. My grandmother played piano and had a pleasant alto voice. My mother had a beautiful coloratura soprano voice and was a fantastic dancer. I loved seeing her sing and dance around the house and sing with the church choir. She was too introverted to want to perform solos in front of others, but she encouraged me to take piano lessons and voice lessons.

In her forties, she had surgery for uterine cancer, and lived a healthy life for many years after passing her five-year cure period. As she approached her eighties, the effects of cigarettes began to take a toll on her. She had a stroke but was able to fully recover. She did stop smoking after that. Shortly after that, she had pulmonary problems with hardening of the arteries and poor circulation. Finally, in July of 2013, when she was almost 89, she was diagnosed with terminal bladder cancer. The doctors predicted she would live about six to nine months.

Several months before my mother is diagnosed with bladder cancer, *I have a dream that she is walking through the massive building at McLean Bible church with me. We go through the first room and it is dark and burning hot and I know it is symbolizing hell. We continue walking and it is average temperature and neutral surroundings, which feels like we are on earth, and when we get to the final room, I look in the window and Mary is holding her arms out to my mother, who immediately goes to Mary, and I know she is taking her to heaven. My first thought is "No! Don't go!", but I realize this is where she can be out of pain and at peace forever, and I will be with her again.* I will continue to have frequent dreams, revealing information, that continue after my mom dies.

My siblings, Danny, Maureen and I try to spend as much time as possible with her. My other sibling, Anne, lives in Reno. My mom and I talk, and I ask her about her sending a sign, when she enters heaven. She tells me she will send the sign through a bird, who is her favorite animal, because birds can sing and can fly away when they are ready to leave.

When we are with her, we share fond memories and ask what we can do for her. She says she would like my daughter Holly and I to sing the song "Heart of Jesus", which she sang with her mother and she also sang with me. Holly, who is shy, learns it and agrees to sing it just for her, but doesn't want anyone else there. The day comes to sing it, and my mom, who hasn't sung in years, and has barely been talking, joins in the last verse and has tears of joy in her eyes. Fortunately, I taped it, and have listened over and over to remember the three of us singing together.

We celebrate her 89th birthday. She is in increasing pain, as the cancer spreads through her body, and often sits in her chair and softly moans. It breaks our hearts, so we talk her into a doctor visit, so we can have him prescribe morphine, and once he does, she agrees to take it. My niece, Maureen and Bob come to visit, and Maureen, sensing her grandmother won't be here much longer, decides to stay to help care for her, but Bob needs to get back to his job in Ohio. She is wonderfully patient and loving to mom. She stays to help care for her until she passes.

Though hospice has told us she is not showing the signs of the end of life yet, and will likely live for several more weeks, *I wake up four days before she dies, hearing a thought in my right ear, "Cathy your mother only has days left"*. I am stunned at the news, and unsure if I should do anything, as I wonder if I am crazy. I decide it really did occur, and I should let my mom know when Anne is coming. The next day, I tell my mom that my sister has a flight to come in five days, and she really wants time with her before she passes. She says, "Well, you'd better to tell her to come sooner." We call my sister, Anne, to tell her that she'd better come now. She arrives from Reno the following day, and a few hours after seeing my sister, my mom goes into a coma.

We all pray the rosary around her and sing Ave Maria and Heart of Jesus, her two favorite hymns. Though she can't speak, she squeezes my hand, so I know she hears us. Early the next morning, she sits up abruptly with her arms out and a smile on her face, takes her last breath, and goes to heaven. When we all gather at her house that afternoon, on November 6th, 2013, and sit outside, it is a nice sunny fall day. Suddenly, there are ladybugs coming all over the patio, and as we go inside, there are several ladybugs at the table where we all sit around to try to eat dinner.

In the fifteen years she has lived there, none of us has ever seen a ladybug in the hundreds of times we have been to her home. I think it is odd, but don't think too much more of it. However, over the next few days, everyone in our family is mentioning they are seeing ladybugs all over the place. I google ladybugs, and read that in the middle ages, farmers had trouble with insects eating their crops and prayed to the Virgin Mary to help. They named the bugs Beetles of our Lady, because these bugs eat plant-eating insects, and they saved the crops, and they became known as Ladybugs.

Ladybugs still show up on our important family dates and events and remind us that Our Lady sends us her grace and favor. My mother died only four months after she is diagnosed but being able to spend time with her near the end of her life and seeing her in such pain made it easier to release her to heaven. Many signs are sent at the end of her illness and continue to the present day.

When looking through my mom's belongings after she passes, I find a book I had given her 20 years earlier, on the life of Mary and the rosary, entitled *A Woman Clothed with the Sun—Eight Great Apparitions of Our Lady*. It is edited and copyrighted by John J. Delaney. It is a beautiful book. I have a dream that my mom tells me to find the blue rosary. I look and find the blue rosary from Lourdes. I begin praying the rosary every day. After a few months, it becomes a special routine, that is my favorite time of day. I wake up at 5:30 to have a cup of coffee and say the rosary and spend some time in prayer, before I wake Keith to get ready for school at 6:15. It makes me feel more connected to my mother in heaven and to our heavenly mother, Mary.

In the book *Jesus and the Jewish Roots of Mary*, by Brant Pitre, in the final chapter, "At the Foot of the Cross", he states on the last page that "once we begin to take Mary as our mother, you learn she has already been there waiting for you with arms open to obey Jesus' last words to "Behold your mother and take her to be your own."[1] I find it so comforting that in the dream I described of my mother and Mary, I saw Mary had her arms open to take my mother to heaven. What about you? Will you accept her grace, and pray her rosary for your sins and the sins of the world, and thank her for her grace and intercession on behalf of her son, our Lord, Jesus Christ?

I have had many times in my sessions of prayer when I have also felt called to pray for, volunteer and support ending abortion. I feel this is part of the message that I am called to bring to people. I believe that life begins at conception and that God should have the sole power of giving life and of taking life. We can and should support mothers and fathers in having and raising these babies. It is another example of surrendering our human power to God's will and obeying. The choice for humans comes before the act of creation of life.

God knew us and loved us before we were born, and His unconditional love is with us from before we were born through eternity. I also believe that the sacred heart of Jesus is broken when women, who are honored with carrying life, choose to abort this life, whom God has given as a sacred and precious gift. It is not choosing an act of love, by destroying this new life, because we don't want the responsibility. There is also the choice to give the baby to someone else who desperately wants to have this baby and raise the child.

Just to get some sense of the amount of abortions, I looked up statistics on legal abortions since 1973 to 2004 and it is 44,000,000.[2] I also looked up the amount of deaths from wars since our country was founded until 2004, and the amount is 1, 109,000.[3] Granted, 2004 was a long time ago, and statistics have changed since then, so it is not an accurate figure in 2020. I must conclude, though, that there have been even more abortions than deaths from war in that time. Especially since the figure from abortions are only

1. Pitre, *Jesus and the Jewish Roots of Mary*, 192.
2. Nrlc.org, *Abortion Statistics*.
3. Wikipedia.org, *US War Casualties*.

the legal abortions that are reported. This is a staggering amount of lost lives.

By the same token, I believe that we should not take life of sick, disabled or elderly into our hands, but rather support that life as lovingly as possible, until God takes that life into his loving care. I think we should support these lives with care, money, service, prayers and another other way that we are able. If every person gave of themselves a small amount, this could be achieved. I have found that it is often those who have the least resources to give that have the biggest hearts. I know that many people do not agree with me, but this is a very important issue to me that I stand by.

Prayer: "Hail Mary"

Song: "Heart of Jesus, Meek and Mild" unknown composer

Bible quote: Psalm 121 "The Lord watches over you. The Lord is your shade at your right hand . . . The Lord will watch over your coming and going both now and forevermore."

9

More Learning

2015–2017

AT THE THERAPEUTIC REC (TREC) summer program, just a few weeks before school begins, Keith tosses a checker piece in air and catches it in his mouth. It becomes lodged in his throat. The staff doesn't realize he has swallowed it and sends him home on the bus. By the time he arrives, he is foaming at the mouth and having difficulty breathing. *Earl and I are praying "Lord help our son, Jesus!"* as he is taken to the hospital. As they are about to do a tracheotomy, Earl sees the panic in his eyes and whistles his "It's OK buddy" signal. Keith tries to take a deep breath to return the whistle, and the checker piece comes dislodged as he tries to whistle back. We are stunned with this breath that Keith takes in, as we release the breath we have been holding in and can now release in relief! *Amen Jesus!*

After a few days, when we see Keith is physically OK, we calm down a bit. He does only want to eat liquid food for quite a few days, as the spot in his throat is irritated. The doctors say he may have a spot that stays irritated for quite some time. I do call the staff at TREC, to notify them of the event and let them know why Keith will not be returning. I stress the importance of making sure that staff are trained to be observant enough to notice things when they should not happen and take action to keep everyone safe. They agree, and let me know staff will be talked to, and future staff will be trained to include that safety procedure.

Keith begins at high school, and we start the school year with the hope that he will settle down into a better routine. Though most of the staff is hard working and caring, the attention to tracking data for behavior and adjusting strategies is not done in an efficient and timely manner. There is one staff member there who is wonderful, but she does not have Keith in her class. She realized Keith's potential and presented him with a citizen's award at the end of the year. This is the first award or recognition he had gotten since elementary school. We were all so proud of him and cheered when his name was called.

When things are no better by the following school year, we hold a meeting, and he transfers to a Center. The excellent staff and consistency in routine allow him to settle down and bit by bit he improves, until his appropriate behavior allows him to become more independent and begin working at job sites. The staff there is amazingly professional and compassionate and communicates daily on Keith's progress. The entire team deserve a big kudos!

Also, during this time, one of the new members of our bible study behaves in an extremely unkind manner to the person who invited her to join. It hurts me so badly to see this continue to happen. I don't find the same joy in attending the meetings. *I pray to God for direction, and very clearly hear his command to continue attending the meetings, because the meetings are not about my comfort, but about obeying His will.* Choosing His will provides the best opportunity for His love to be revealed in our life. When I attend the following session, I am told that this person will no longer attend. As always, God is a step ahead of me.

In May of 2017, I attend a Christian woman's seminar. One of the presenters at the seminar is Laura Story, a Christian speaker and composer. She speaks about how despite a tragedy in her life, she has chosen to live with the joy Christ has given her. She performs the song *Blessings*, which I have listed as the song at the end of Chapter Ten.

The week after the seminar, I am to have Mohs surgery performed on my forehead for squamous cell carcinoma. I am nervous, as it is my first time with a cancer diagnosis. I remember thinking, *"Oh, God, it was so nice of you to let me hear this song and be comforted right before my surgery."* As I was driving in the pouring rain on the way to have the surgery, I am going around a sharp curve, and a large truck slams his brakes, and misses slamming into the drivers' door of my car by inches. I heard the voice in my mind say, *"Do not be afraid. I am with you."* and knew whatever happened, I would be fine.

As so often happens, God had additional, more important plans for that song. A few days after the seminar, one of our closest family friends called to let me know that her daughters' husband had passed away. He was only in his early thirties. It was sudden, and they were devastated. She asked me if I could sing, and if there was any special song that would comfort their family. Of course, I knew right away that the Lord intended for me to sing *Blessings*. I did sing it, and it was very comforting to them. I know it was no coincidence in the timing that I was presented with this song. I was invited to sing for parents at a Jill's House retreat, and the song seemed so perfect there as well.

Prayer: "Apostles' Creed"

Song: "Ave Maria" Franz Schubert

Bible quote: Isaiah 40:31 "We are hard pressed on every side, but not crushed."

10

A Choice to Just Breathe in His Presence

2018–2020

MY OLDEST DAUGHTER, TARA, who lives in Seattle, and has two boys, ages three and six, is diagnosed with breast cancer in May of 2018. We are all so afraid for her. The biggest fear of every parent is having their child die. I am angry at God. I think "God, didn't we agree that I would do anything for you but lose a living child? I had two miscarriages. I had children with disabilities. My mother had died. This was not part of the deal! Why isn't it me with cancer instead?!"

We pray and are comforted to remember, *"Be not afraid. I am always with you."* She has a mastectomy, and they discover it is in her lymph nodes. She has a second surgery to remove the lymph nodes, followed by chemotherapy, then radiation. Through all of this, Tara has a positive attitude and focuses on getting healed and appreciating every day of her life. If she can do this, even though she is the one enduring this difficult journey, with the grace of Christ, I surely can do this too. For her, for Him, I will do this. I will be positive and helpful, appreciative, and most of all, loving.

I am happy to be with them to help, but feel like I am totally depleted, from trips back and forth to help with care of Tara and my grandsons. This, on top of forty years of caretaking for others, while still caring for Keith and working two jobs has taken a toll on my health. I have lost energy, am not sleeping well and find that I get sick a lot. As I pray, reflect and meditate, I begin to feel re-charged. I feel a bit stronger, more energized and healthier. I feel like I can go on, but it is a reminder that I need to take care of myself first in order to care for my family and students.

In June, I stop my position as youth choir director and on the way home from the last Sunday directing there, I stop by our neighborhood church, to say a prayer to ask God where I am going to go to church now, that I can still have music be a special part of service. On my way out, I pick up the bulletin and see that there is a new pastor coming, and a new choir director. This seems like the perfect opportunity to return to this parish, and this time I can just volunteer and have my daughter, Holly, sing with me. I look forward to beginning in the fall.

In February of 2019, Keith gets the flu, which sends him to the hospital, and while caring for him, I get the flu, then bronchitis. While I have a high fever, I am in an almost delirious state, and resting in my bed, I dream God is telling me he wants me to take a long rest. It is a rest I have needed for too long, that I have wanted for so long. I did not allow myself to take care of the caretaker, until God showed me, and I am only too happy to obey. I go back to work, but I do not fully recover my strength and my singing voice until April. I begin to think that the time for my career as a special education teacher is coming to an end, unless I can find a way to re-charge myself and say no to some requests for assistance.

In the summer of 2019, we go visit Tara and the family, to celebrate that she has finished two surgeries, chemotherapy and radiation. It is a visit full of appreciation of her healthy and full life and our ability to share it with her and her family. It is the beginning of a new and better year, where Tara will be able to return to teaching and her "normal" life, and where my daughter Heather plans her wedding and new married life in summer of 2020. It is time for me to take a break from teaching. It is a time to reflect, take care of myself and family and decide what my next step should be. I have been so busy caring for others for forty years, I realize this is the first time I can choose what I want to do, and I enjoy that thought. It is a time I need to choose what I should be doing. It is a time I need to hear God's re-direction.

I take a leave of absence from the 2019–2020 school year. I am so grateful for the support of my boss, and the principal of the high school where I teach. It allows me time to make a visit to take care of Tara and my grandsons, for her reconstructive surgery and recovery. It allows me to have the energy to take care of Keith. It allows me to make choices about days to sub and times to do activities for myself or friends and family members. Meanwhile, as the gentleness of Mary surrounds me more every day that I pray and say the rosary, I want to do more to help the pro-life cause. I begin to attend meetings at our pro-life group at church, and at the Divine Mercy events. I stand in unity with other volunteers to pray the rosary at abortion clinics.

In the Spring of 2019, I feel called to take up the cross and share this story of the love of Christ being the only important thing in this life and for eternal life. I feel Jesus ask, "Cathy do you love me?" and I immediately think "Yes, Jesus, I love you!" Then I sense Jesus asking, "Will you carry my cross?" I was stunned and had no idea what Jesus meant. I was silent. I felt it again. "Do you love me?" My reply "Yes Jesus!" The question, "Will you carry my cross?" My reply "I don't know what you mean Lord!" The third time, "Do you love me?" My reply "I love you Jesus!" Again "Will you carry my cross?" Finally, "Yes, Lord, I will carry your cross, but how will I know what you want me to do?!" The answer, "It will be revealed to you."

I seem to read and hear things about "Carrying the Cross" in sermons and bible-study sessions that I hadn't heard or paid attention to much before. I wonder if I imagined all that went on in my calling. I talk to our choir-director at church about it, because he is such a faith-filled, knowledgeable and caring person and I know he would keep our conversation to himself. He is supportive, confirms I am not crazy, and offers a book to read, *The 10 Universal Principles: Brief Philosophy of Life Issues*, by Robert J. Spitzer, S.J. I pray and read the book. I read the book and find it very helpful in supporting my faith and for discussion points to talk to other people about my faith, and possibly to help support them in their journey of faith. I also talk to our pastor. He tells me that even though it is Jesus' timing to reveal his plans, it is okay to ask him to help me know his will and obey. I realize that these events that have happened have been a part of Jesus' plan in preparing me for this journey.

In December of 2019, I know this is the time to begin the book. I realize this is more than just my life story book. It needs to be a book about sharing the love of Jesus and Mary I have had in my life with others and encouraging them to choose to do the same. It is also about guiding and supporting people to follow through on making this choice, by making time to pray and reflect on what this means in your life. It will be a different path for each of us, but equally as important to you as to me, and eternally as important to you and to Jesus and Mary.

I have difficulty deciding the exact title of the book but know that Carrying the Cross is important. I submit the book outline that the publisher requires and wait to see if it is accepted. Meanwhile, I make the decision to work on it every day and have faith that if, and when God wants it to be accepted, it will be. If not, I will share it with my family and friends. If it helps one person to see the light of Christ, and pick up the cross, it is worth the effort.

As I close this chapter in my book, I am preparing to take a trip to Seattle to be with Tara and two grandsons to help with care after her reconstructive surgery. I am helping my family make plans to help my brother, Danny, the oldest of siblings, with end of life plans, as his health begins to deteriorate. I am working with Earl on getting the house ready to put on the market. I am singing in two choirs and making plans on continuing some type of work with Fairfax County. So, hardly "retiring", but enjoying my choices and continuing to pray daily to God to help me to hear and obey his will. I pray you live your life fully, hearing and obeying his will, by simply calling *"Jesus, be with me."*

Prayer: The Rosary was given by Mary to St. Dominic. At the beginning of each of the 5 decades of beads the Our Father is prayed, followed by ten Hail Mary's, and at the end of each decade, the Glory Be is prayed. There are Five Joyful Mysteries; Five Luminous Mysteries; Five Sorrowful Mysteries; Five Glorious Mysteries. You meditate on the parts to the mystery as you pray each decade.

Song: "Blessings" by Laura Story

Bible quote: Romans 8:28 "And we know that in all things God works for the good of those who love him, who have been called according to his purpose."

11

Trip to Seattle

As I BEGIN TO prepare for my trip to Seattle, I pray daily to Jesus to prepare me spiritually, mentally and physically. I ask him to send the Holy Spirit to guide me to seek the presence of Jesus in every moment of every day. I pray that every thought, word and deed is done in his honor and glory. I pray that I will not be anxious, but instead, will be able to appreciate every moment of the sixteen days I will be with my daughter, son-in-law and grandchildren. I pray that I stay healthy and sleep well, which I often have trouble doing when I travel away from the comforts of home. I pray that Keith will do well while I am gone, as I have never been away from him for such a long time. Yes, truly, *all these things I pray to Jesus,* knowing I can fully open my heart and say, *"I am confident, I am courageous, I am joyful, for you are always with me Lord."*

I arrive on February 3rd, the day before her reconstructive surgery and am so happy we have some time alone that evening. I am happy to enjoy sitting together and talking about the plans to make her surgery and recovery go as smoothly as possible. The next morning, Patrick goes to the hospital with Tara, and I take the boys to school. After I drop them, I decide to get some breakfast in town, and take a nice long walk alone, since I know my free time will be limited in the days ahead. She will stay in the hospital for two nights. The surgery goes well, and I say a prayer of thanks, *"Lord, thank you for your goodness to Tara! Continue to allow her complete and rapid recovery"*. I do not get to see her that day, as she is in intensive care the first day. I pick the boys up from school and we have a nice evening together, enjoying playtime, homework for Cameron, dinner, a movie, baths and a story for James at bedtime. The following day, after I drop the boys at school, I head to the hospital to visit Tara. She is moved out of intensive care to a room and is stable. She will come home tomorrow. I leave to pick the boys up from school and repeat yesterday's routine. The boys are happy to know mom will be home the next day.

The first week is a strict routine of dispensing and notating four medications round the clock, fixing Tara's drinks and meals, and stripping the three drains. It was important to empty the drains to prevent infection, and to measure the draining amount two or three times a day, in order to be sure that the amount of drainage was reducing. Patrick took on most of these caretaking duties for Tara. I need to add that everything he did for her was done with a smile and a loving touch. They both slept in the living room, as Tara needed to sit up when sleeping, to reduce chance of getting pneumonia after surgery. She was also not allowed to walk up the stairs or lift her arms, as her stitches were in both the upper and lower section of the body. I also need to add that Tara never complained, and followed orders to a tee, though she was in a great deal of pain the first week. Their teamwork was endearing to see and made me appreciate even more being a part of the team.

I had caretaking duties for my grandsons the first week and loved every minute of the day. I got to sleep upstairs in the comfortable bed. I had my rosary to pray every night as I fell asleep and time to have my cup of coffee and say my prayers in the morning before I began the day. The three hour later Pacific time difference worked in my favor, as I was exhausted by bedtime, and had no trouble sleeping after my rosary.

I also was able to wake up very early to keep my routine in the morning before the boys got up for school. I helped the boys get breakfast and get dressed, then dropped them at school. Each day after I dropped them at school, I did an errand to pick up some necessary items, came back and sat with Tara and watched Anne of Green Gables series, had lunch with her, took a walk in the neighborhood and enjoyed the serene and beautiful nature.

They live about a half hour drive from Seattle, in the green hills of Issaquah. Before I knew it, it was time to pick up the boys and let them have a snack, play outside, do homework, make dinner and clean up, watch a show, sing some songs or play a game, and get ready for bed. After the boys went to bed, I was able to read, do a puzzle or watch a show.

As the first week ended, Earl came out for a few days to visit Tara and help with our grandsons. He took them swimming at the indoor pool, to the Donut Shop, to McDonalds and helped with chores around the house. We all went to the zoo, where I was amazed at seeing some animals I had never seen in person, such as penguins and kangaroos and elk. It is easy to see God's presence so clearly in the miracles of nature. The balance of the power and tenderness of God is revealed so perfectly in nature.

It is only when we slow down enough to notice and absorb these miracles that we can fully appreciate them. I would never choose to be in this circumstance of having my daughter in reconstructive surgery, but sometimes when we can't control the circumstances, but can control our choices in how to react to them, that is the best we can do. So, I chose to fully embrace being in this time and place, with love and hope.

By then, we had a houseful of people to feed, clean and clothe. So, we had lots of dishes and loads of laundry, vacuuming and scrubbing bathrooms to do. Earl left and Patrick went back to work, so I would work all these tasks in between taking and picking up the boys. At this time, Tara went back for her week followup after surgery, and all was going well, so she was able to move around more and in less pain. The boys and I went to Sammamish state park a few times, where they could be in the outdoors and use up all their energy. When my head hit the pillow every night, I was so appreciative to have been blessed to be a part of supporting my family. When Valentine's Day neared, Cameron and I went together to pick some candy and cards to bring to school. We stopped and got a special box of chocolates to bring home for mom and dad.

I was especially aware of the joy of being both a mother and grandmother during this time. During many of my prayer sessions, my heart was filled with love for Mary, the mother of Jesus, who became the mother to all mankind. Jesus specifically asked her to take this role in the moments before he died on the cross. She had the honor and heartbreak, the grief and joy, in choosing to carry the cross of being the mother to Jesus. By agreeing to also be the mother of all of mankind, she opened her heart to carry the cross for all mankind.

Mary has appeared numerous times to ask people to pray the rosary. When I pray the rosary, I begin with my own prayer, which I have listed below. I have also listed three of my favorite songs about Mary that I have sung for many years. Mary asks for prayers for her son Jesus, and acts as intercessor for these prayers. She encourages us to pray for our sins to be forgiven, so that we are closer to Jesus in our earthly life and will be with him in eternal life in heaven.

Tara and I had some wonderful conversations that I will always carry in my heart. We were able to plan for her sister, Heather's upcoming wedding in June. We got some great pictures, that I carry on my phone and memories I have stored in my mind. I could not believe how quickly February 18th arrived, and it was time to come home. As much as a part of me hated to leave, I was content that Tara was doing well and had recovered enough to be more independent.

I was grateful for the time there, and ready to come back to the rest of my family that I had missed so much. This was a special gift and I am so happy that God allowed me to embrace this trip as I was embraced. I was looking forward to getting back and submitting my manuscript for publication. My prayers were of all praise of the hope, peace and grace Jesus and Mary had provided. Little did I imagine the health pandemic that was to begin only days upon my return, and how my world and the world of everyone would change.

Prayer: I offer your rosary for my sins and the sins of the world, and thank you for the grace of your intercession, on behalf of your son, our Lord, Jesus Christ.

Songs: "Hail Holy Queen", "Immaculate Mary", "The Angel Gabriel from Heaven Came"

Bible Quote: John 15:13 "Greater love has no one than this: to lay down one's life for one's friends."

12

Coronavirus and More

I TOOK A FEW days to gradually work my life back into my world waiting for me upon my return home. The following week, I had sub jobs several days. On Friday, Heather and I went to Virginia Beach to finalize plans for her wedding, which is June 27th. We also had plans for a bridal shower and a bachelorette trip to N.Y. city. I was offered a long-term sub position, beginning March 9th, and lasting through the end of the school year. It felt like the perfect timing, because I was done with my trips to Seattle for the foreseeable future and would have more time and energy. I liked the balance of the excitement of a new position, with the comfort of the being at the same school I had been working before I took a year's leave of absence. Earl and I talked, and I prayed, and I decided to take the position in the morning.

As I awoke the morning after the offer of the sub position, and began my prayers, I sensed an urgency to get the book completed. It felt like I needed to get everything in order to submit now. I wasn't sure why there was an urgency but followed the plan I believed Jesus was sending me. On March 12, I received an offer of publication. Of course, I was ecstatic that there would be people who could share in my story about the love of Jesus and carrying

His cross. I knew this needed to be focus of the book, because it was what I had heard repeated to me three times before I knew exactly what this book would be about or what the title would be. I am humbled and honored to be able to help bring as many people as possible closer to our Lord.

The more you surround yourself with time with Jesus in prayer, song, mass, bible-study, and the sacraments, the more your heart opens to obey the Lord's will. If you have something you think you are called to do for God, prepare your heart, mind and soul by spending time with him. Add actions into your life, such as volunteering or working in an area you can contribute your talent to help others. Sometimes God's plans may be delivered as a loud wake-up call, and sometimes they may be a subtle whisper. If your actions are done in the love of Christ, for his honor and glory, you will know you are following God's plans.

I was amazed again at the timing of God. I had been back to teaching only a week, when we got notice that schools would close, on March 13th, due to the Coronavirus. Initially, the closure was to be for a few weeks. Of course, each day, the news grimmer, with details of sickness and death. I also realized that I had just been in the Seattle area a week before it had hit Seattle. Keith has a compromised immune system, so I have had to make sure he is home, except for taking walks, and that only his immediate family is in the home. Earl, being a police officer, still needs to go to work, but is vigilant about washing his hands and limiting contact.

I have chosen to hear the minimal amount of news—just enough to stay on top of the actions to take to stay healthy. With the social distancing order that has been given, I am not able to go to choir rehearsal or service, so I was very pleased when our choir director sent me a link to the Catholic Diocese, listing online access to services, prayers and music. I pray the rosary while watching the priest pray at Lourdes, asking for healing for those who have been sick from the Coronavirus and peace from the worries the virus has caused.

I have surrounded myself with prayers and music from station EWTN. I enjoyed a concert with the Orchestra of Paris performing

Faure's "Requiem". It helps lessen the absence of connection with the community and is much more peaceful than surrounding myself with media coverage. I also vocalize and take a walk by myself every morning before Earl goes to work, and I am alone for care of Keith. I read and FaceTime with my children and grandchildren.

We have stayed in the same daily school routine, as consistency is helpful for Keith. He goes to bed, wakes, and eats his meals at the same time as if he were in school. He takes a walk with me every afternoon and we talk about his day and his interests, such as what is for dinner and the eagles, dogs and cardinals we see. It is a simple but beautiful way to spend the day, appreciating the innocent way he sees life and lives his day. I especially think of this, on March 21st, which is World Down Syndrome Day.

In my prayers, I see Jesus in the Divine Mercy picture I have in my mind, after reading of Saint Faustina and her encounters with Jesus, requesting she let people know that Jesus wanted to offer His Divine Mercy to sinners. He instructed her to tell people about the Chaplet of Divine Mercy, where all sinners can receive grace from Jesus. She became the patron saint of mercy, devoting her life to this mission to honor Jesus and helping people be united with Jesus on earth and for eternity in heaven.

I hesitated to end my book on the topic of the Coronavirus. It is such a world changing event that has just begun and is changing daily. There is such uncertainty and fear right now. A simple song I find so comforting is "The Light of Christ" by Marty Haugen. It calms my mind and soul to remember that Christ's light is constant. It does not depend on situations and circumstances. It is always here to guide us and bring us to His love. Right now, the world is in a time of trying to find the treasures of the moments of the present and balancing them with the preparation of the unknown future. It is also a season of moving from winter to spring and of Lent to Easter.

In nature, winter sheds the old blankets we have needed, to allow the new growth to happen from the seeds that had been planted before winter. It is a time of abundance of rain and sunshine, to balance what is necessary for new growth. It is an out with the old and in with the new. We let go because we know this is a natural occurrence that happens annually, and it is a process of growth.

Similarly, the passage of Lent to Easter in Christianity begins with darkness and uncertainty as we begin our forty days of Lent. It is a time for reflection of our lives, and an opportunity to prepare for confession of sins and forgiveness. It is an opportunity to move from the weight of heaviness of our sins to lightness of forgiveness of these sins. We need only to choose Jesus as our Savior, in order to begin our new life on earth and to share eternal life with Jesus in heaven. This choice is open to each person, through the grace and divine mercy of Christ.

Our choir director sent us a list of traditional Catholic hymns that provide faith, trust and providence, that I'd like to share with you, in the hope that it uplifts you in these difficult days.

> All People that on Earth Do Dwell
> I Sing the Mighty Power of God
> O God, Our Help in Ages Past
> Be Still My Soul
> How Firm a Foundation
> Lord of All Hopefulness
> Take Up Thy Cross
> Be Thou My Vision
> God is My Great Desire
> All Things Bright and Beautiful
> The King of Love My Shepherd Is
> Lord Jesus, Think on Me
> Let All Things Now Living
> Now Thank We All Our God

One of my favorite hymns about reflection and opening our hearts to Jesus is *Create in Me, Oh God* by Johannes Brahms, which is based on Psalm 51. I suggest you listen to it and see if it lightens your heart and your mood and allows you to have a contrite heart that is open to receiving God's blessings. Another favorite of mine is Mendelssohn's *He, Watching Over Israel* from his Oratorio, *Elijah*. He re-assures us that Christ never stops watching over us, and no matter what grief we have, he is by our side to comfort us.

Heather, Holly and Craig were the siblings who were living at home and had the most interaction with Keith. He affected their lives in such a positive way. He has taught all three of them the qualities of patience, perseverance, tenderness and compassion. Heather got her degree in special education so that she could help other people with disabilities and their families. She takes Keith on social and community outings weekly. Craig took Keith to countless riding lessons, baseball and basketball practices. Craig and Holly both have helped in Keith's care and babysitting for him when Earl and I go out together. They would all tell you that Keith has improved their lives ten times over the amount they have improved his life.

It has allowed all three of them to be more aware of people who need help, and of reaching out to help when they can. It has also motivated them and guided them in their choice of careers. We can all learn from these young adults. Reaching out to others with compassion, even when we really don't have the energy, time, or money is one of the biggest ways we can show the love of Jesus. Jesus asks us to love our neighbor as ourselves. Passing on acts of kindness, with no expectation of anything in return, is helpful to others and it is helpful to ourselves.

The other thing we did while raising our children, was to demonstrate and discuss with them the importance of living a life with God, family and country as their priorities. As humans, we tend to assume our lives are going to go along the way they always have, and that we want them to go. We also assume we can control these circumstances. The coronavirus has been a heartbreaking, but true example of the lack of total control we have and need for placing our trust in Christ. Many of us have already chosen to reach out to help and to trust in doing the best we can each day to follow the guidelines for quarantines, social distancing and hand washing.

We have seen thousands of heroes step up to help total strangers. We have seen millions of people re-thinking the priorities in their lives. It is much easier to show love to people we love. It is especially challenging to reach out to strangers or people we don't love. Is your heart open? Can you find one act a week to reach out to someone who needs your help? You will be glad you did!

Between March 21st and April 1st, the world cases have gone from 33,180 to 906,764 and deaths have gone from 12,944 to 45,408. In the United States, the total cases are now 199,890 and deaths are now 4,380.[1] I give you these statistics just to let you know that this is a rapidly growing and changing pandemic. Social distancing, hand washing and one-day-at-a-time has become the norm for trying to slow down the growth of this monster.

As it became larger and larger, the schools closed through the end of the school year. Plans were created for teachers to devise on-line learning for students. Teachers worked diligently and met online to be ready to begin teaching students on-line, after Spring break on April 14th. It is challenging, because many teachers have their children home with them while working, but it is just the way it needs to be, and everyone is supporting one another.

Everyone is doing the best they can do to take one day at a time, appreciating being healthy and having their loved ones be healthy, as the main priority. They are also trying to work in some mental, physical and spiritual health through whatever are the most helpful ways. Many people have lost their income, and the federal government has devised a plan to give payment to families to help get through the crisis.

It almost feels like a bad dream that you go to sleep to every night, praying your loved ones stay healthy and appreciate the gifts they have every day. But when you wake up each morning, your first thought is that it isn't a bad dream, it's a reality that makes you sigh, take a deep breath, say a prayer and know you will repeat again today, and the next day, and many more days to come. Still, somehow, with strength from God, you can go on. You can laugh at something silly with your child. You can help a neighbor get groceries. You can help a stranger by sending an inspiring message or video. You can make a phone call or send a letter to someone who is lonely.

---

1. CNN.Com, *Covid-19 Updates.*

Somehow you try new aspects of your old routine, and find out what is helpful, and embrace that, while tossing out things that aren't helpful with the new situation. Since Keith and I are home every day all day long, and he needs assistance or at least an eye watching over almost everything he does, I have a new routine for our days that incorporate that into our time at home together. Our routine includes making a chart of options for each day together every morning, which includes choosing meals, school and chore activities, and fun time together.

I work that around the teacher training and planning for online classes and household activities, and personal things I need and choose to do. I love waking up and having my cup of coffee and prayer time alone, having time with Keith and time to complete my things, getting a walk alone every morning and hearing the birds, and walking again with Keith in the late afternoons and chatting with him about his day. Singing is a great form of prayer that is good for the body and soul. It doesn't matter if you are a great singer or not. You can sing at the top of your lungs in your shower. When my day is done, I am happy to lay my head on my pillow in grateful prayer and go to sleep peacefully.

I can stay in a semi-normal world here at home, surrounded by many comforts and routines. Earl goes to work every day, seeing all the changes in people and places, as he drives and walks around his assigned location at the airport. He must be vigilant to everyone's safety in and around the airport. He must endure changes made every day on guidelines of what to do and what not to do and changes in schedules. He must answer questions and interact with people coming and going from flights. Yesterday when he was working, he and another officer stopped a citizen to investigate his involvement in carjacking . The citizen became agitated and spit on them. He changed his uniform and washed up with soap and water, but there is concern the coronavirus may be brought home to our family. Still, we are grateful he has an income, and pray he remains healthy, as so many people in the world are doing.

We are especially concerned that if Keith contracts the virus, he may not have a strong enough immune system to survive the virus. The interferon response in his immune system is activated constantly, instead of only activating when they fight an infection, as in typical people, so it is at a constant level of depletion, and not able to fight infection as well. Earl and Holly have limited their contact in the community and with Keith, since they are out working. They have told me that they keep in the back of their mind the thought that if they make a mistake of not washing hands one time or getting too close to Keith, it would be their fault if Keith gets it. At this time, we are not even having his other brother and sister come into the house, in order to keep the possibility at the lowest possible chance.

Earl and I have always prayed with and for our family, our community and our country. Now, we know it is even more important to pray. We know it is not true that there is nothing we can do. We can all pray. We all pray daily, sometimes multiple times a day. It is important to start by making it a daily priority for each of us. We pray by ourselves, as it opens our hearts to Jesus to praise him for dying on the cross for our sins, to ask for his protection and peace, and to spend time with him.

We pray as a family, saying the rosary together, saying a pray before we go to work for blessings for the day, or a prayer before we go to bed for gratitude for the day. We pray in the neighborhood with bible study online or online emails. We pray with the country, in online masses, rosary, stations of the cross. The prayer for world peace begins in our own homes with our families. St. Francis believed that Jesus calls us to help our neighbors whenever possible, and patiently, gently and humbly spent his lifetime following Christ. Every time we help someone else, we help Christ carry His cross. Edmund Burke, the Irish statesman and philosopher said, "All that is necessary for evil to triumph is for good to do nothing."[2] We have seen this evidenced in history.

Though it is more difficult to do now, with social distancing because of the Coronavirus, in addition to prayer, we can take action that makes a difference. We can help protect and support the more vulnerable population. We can seek the unborn, the elderly,

2. Burke, *Thoughts*, 82.

the disabled, the homeless and give our love, time, energy and money in so many ways. Prayer and actions do make a difference, in our lives and in lives of others. We must be soldiers in Christ to fight for this opportunity. We can choose to follow the good shepherd, who is the king of love. Taking an action of love will change the course of history.

On Palm Sunday, we begin Holy Week that leads to the Tridium of Holy Thursday, Good Friday, Holy Saturday and Easter. On Holy Thursday, Jesus washes clean the feet of the disciples, and performs the sacrament of Eucharist, at the last supper. On Good Friday, Jesus was persecuted and crucified. While hanging on the cross during his final hours of life, Jesus revealed both his humanity and divinity. In the gospels of the disciples Matthew, Mark, Luke and John, the final words of Jesus are revealed. Jesus asked God for forgiveness for those who crucified him; Jesus told the criminal hanging next to him that his faith allowed him to be in paradise with Jesus; Jesus told Mary and the disciples that she is now their mother; Jesus cried out to God, asking why God had forsaken him; He stated he was thirsty; He stated his obedience when he said it is finished; He showed complete trust in God, by committing his spirit to God. Jesus is put in the tomb, surrounded by guards.

In Luke 19:42–44, he states that Jesus spoke to the people, saying "If you, even you, had known on this day what would bring you peace, but now it is hidden from your eyes. You did not recognize the time of God's coming to you." What God promised us is happening right now in the middle of all crisis. Even in the middle of the Coronavirus. Our plans are put on hold. God's plans are still going on. God is going to use this time, as he always does, for the good of all his people.

We may not see any or all of it now, but in our faith, we can believe and trust in his perfect plan. Jesus rises on Easter morning, and completes the plan of God's redemption of all mankind. As we move through our daily crosses, lent, and even the Coronavirus, I pray we rejoice on Easter day and every day, Alleluia! He is Risen! Amen. Paul says in 1Corinthians:13, "And now these three remain: faith, hope, and love. But the greatest of these is love."

As I close this book, I choose to continue to carry my crosses through the love of Jesus Christ. I know this involves times of darkness, filled with pain and grief. I also know that the grace and mercy of Jesus provides joy of eternal life that is always present. My faith in Jesus is what allows me and my brothers and sisters in Christ to rejoice. It is what allows every single person to rejoice. I pray you choose Jesus for yourself. I pray you choose to spread this joy to others, so that they may rejoice too. I pray we may spend eternity together with our Lord, Jesus Christ.

Prayers: Litany of the Sacred Heart of Jesus—St. Margaret Mary Alacoque; Chaplet of Divine Mercy—St. Faustina Kowalska

Songs: "Lift High the Cross"—George William Kitchin; Michael Robert Newbolt; "It Is Well with My Soul"—Horatio Spafford and Philip Bliss; "The King of Love My Shepherd Is"; "Jesus Christ is Risen Today"—Samuel Arnold

Bible Quote: Romans 12:10 "Be devoted to one another in love. Honor one another above yourselves."

Bibliography

Burke, Edmund. *Thoughts on the Cause of the Present Discontents.* London: Macmillan, 1905.

Delaney, John J. *A Woman Clothed with the Sun.* New York: Doubleday, 1995.

Pitre, Brant. *Jesus and the Jewish Roots of Mary.* New York: Image, 2018.

Spitzer, Robert J. *The Ten Universal Principles: Brief Philosophy of Life Issues.* San Francisco: Ignatius, 2011.